JOHN

URBANCIK

ODYSSEY

JOHN
URBANCIK

ODYSSEY

"I have a date..." (page 14) first appeared in *Space & Time* magazine issue #141.

"Give me..." (page 19) first appeared in *Space & Time* magazine issue #139.

DEDICATED TO
THE MEMORY OF
MARY "MERY-ET" LESCHER

I MISS YOU

And now, tell me
and tell me true.
Where have you been
wandering, and in
what countries have
you travelled?
—THE ODYSSEY, HOMER

Her gifts were
mixed with good
and evil both.
—THE ODYSSEY, HOMER

JOHN

URBANCIK

ODYSSEY

What happens
after there are
no more memories
to be made?

My eyes,
    these eyes,
    have seen magic
    and beauty
    and grace.
        And heartbreak.
My hands,
    these hands,
    have held fortunes
    and wishes
    made real.
        And sand.

I drove
to the furthest corners.
I climbed
all the mountains
and forded the rivers.
I danced
with the dancers
and sang
with the singers.
I watched
the sun rise
and I watched
the sun set
a thousand times.
I wrestled
alligators
and swam
with dolphins
and walked alone
down dark city streets.
But since you've gone,
I've felt nothing.

All the devils

    rejoiced

    when you died

    because

    your absence

    made me

    vulnerable.

    But it did not

    make me

    weak,

and the devils

    suffered

    for their mistake.

Don't leave me
   to my thoughts.

My fears
   are greater
   than I
   can face
   alone.

My insecurities
   are loudest
   in the dark.

My hopes
   unfulfilled
   leave me
   panicked
   and weak.

Don't leave me
   to my thoughts.

They run wild
   and ravage
   my heart and
   my head.

Don't leave me.

Perhaps she rides the wind
brushing through your hair
and whispering in your ears.
She's the morning fog
or the clouds at sunset
catching all the red
of the sun.
She's an echo
in the chasm of your heart
where once
she claimed dominion.

Ghosts defy
easy explanation.
That doesn't make her
less substantial.

Don't leave me
just yet,
I beg.
We have dances
yet to dance,
kisses to share,
and unspoken
conversations
on our tongues.
But the sun
has already risen
and my eyes
are already open
and the dream
already fades.

You were never meant
to be alone.
You will always
be haunted.

There are
no directions
for how to
love somebody.
You either do it
until somebody
gets hurt
or somebody dies.

Love and madness are the
same sides of two different
coins. You get one, you get
the other; it's that simple.
So if love isn't driving you to
madness, maybe you better
try the other tactic and let
madness drive you into love.

Today
  I saw a ghost
    but not the ghost
    I wanted to see.
She shimmered,
  made no promises,
  and gave me
    nothing to hope for.
When I tried
  to speak to her,
    she vanished.
I didn't know
  what to say
  anyway.

I stopped to pick up
a traveler on the side of the road.
She said I shouldn't have.
She painted her nails red
as I navigated the highways.
She said she'd been to Vegas
but that was a long time ago
and she didn't care to go back.
She said she'd met a ghost
somewhere near Memphis
but wasn't sure
if it had been real
or a borrowed memory.
I dropped her on the corner
outside a late night bar
where she kissed me once
and told me not to wait.

I have a date
with death.

I'll wear my best cologne
and bring flowers
vibrant and bright—
not black roses,
she never wants those.

I'll take her
to a fancy dinner,
and afterwards dancing.

And if she still
wants to take me
back to her place after,
I'll count myself lucky.

The purpose of poetry:

    To capture a moment,

    a breath — a feeling,

    no matter how fleeting;

    an image, no matter how brief —

    and to share that,

    to better understand

    your own experience,

    to better understand

    your own choices,

    and to better understand yourself.

Dragonfire
and emeralds:
a festive
combination
in winter.

Don't talk to me
of sparrows,
you freak.

Ghosts live
in the silence,
so give them room
to breathe
and maybe
they will reveal
their secrets,
their dreams,
their faces.

I don't know
    if I am the story
    or if the story is me.

Does it flow
    through me
    or from me
    or into me
    from someplace
        unimaginable?

I don't know
    if I am
    the story,
    but the words
    feel like me,
    and I feel
    like the words,
    and the architecture of the story
        may well be my bones.

I don't know
    if the story
    is me,
    but it might also be you.

A single note
on a violin
echoes through
the vastness
of space,
the limits
of time,
but it's
the one note
that
breaks
your heart
over
and
over
again.

The garden snake
only wants to dance,
but if it can't
then maybe it can fly.
It doesn't
breathe fire,
but its forked tongue
only knows
how to lie.

Strolling through
my own shadow fields,
I am often surprised
at the shapes they take
and the sounds they make,
because they often
look like me
and use my voice.

Give me
something
stronger.
Reality
won't leave
me alone.

The map
led him to an oracle
both beautiful and wise.
She spoke
for the goddess of the moon
when she told him to wait.
He was led to a chamber to bathe
and given wine to drink.
At dawn, the goddess returned
in all her splendor
and all her glamour,
but he asked
for the secrets of another's heart.
Roses and orchids,
the moon told him,
and a delicate poison
to apply to his own wounds
should she cut him.
So armed, he called upon his love
under the watchful eye
of a jealous moon.

In a time before gods
and before men,
the emotions
drifted across
the universe,
happy about it,
angry, and afraid.
We still suffer
and revel
in what they learned.

All I want
is a private oasis:
a reading nook
where I can
lounge with my cat,
drink red wine,
and listen
to jazz on vinyl.

From the top
looking down
it all seems so
far away.
The problems,
the fears,
the pain
and misery
drop off into
specks
smaller than
mountains.
It's a long
trek down,
but the road
provides such
scenery.

Always forgetting to breathe,
too focused on where
to find the next
gulp of air.

Blue skies
fall like a blanket
to smother the world
with hope
and even joy,
but the skies
spare no thought
for me.

the ghosts of Midnight
are active
and noisy.
they walk
like whispers
and speak
in shadow
and watch
every
sin
you
make.

Through obscurity
and uncertainty,
through impossible nights
and despite
unimaginable obstacles,
I haven't found
a good place
to give up.

Where is it
    you think
    you are going?

Wherever
        this road
        takes me,
            for starters.

I knew
you had knives.
But I wanted
you to cut me.

Stupid moon
spreading
romance
like candy.

Can I
have some more?

The first thing
I noticed
was how you
looked at me
like I mattered.

When I was younger,
I met a woman
with eyes like
Nordic wildfires.

I didn't know
I'd meet her again.

But in a moment of darkness,
she returned like a goddess,
teasing and tempting,
as is her nature,
then guided me through the dark
like northern lights,
sharing stories of herself
no one's ever known.

There's quicksilver in her veins,
talons in her hands,
and like every great hero,
she's strolled through hell,
but she'll always be safe
with me.

I dare you
to kiss me.
Throw caution
to the wind,
forget all obligations,
enjoy the taste
and savor the passion.
Kiss me
just this one time
and it will never end.
As the heavens collapse
and all the stars fade,
when the universe
falls to oblivion,
all that will remain
will be a monument
to us,
locked eternally
in that one kiss
because you dared.

Kiss me
in the glow of lightning.
It might be the last time.
Maybe we'll get lucky
and it won't.

Give me something
I've never had.
Tell me things unknown
and unimagined.
Break my heart
as if it's never been broken before.

Part demon fae,
you have
infected me.
You have licked
the poison
off my throat
and wrists,
and you liked it.
Part demon fae,
but also part angel,
even if
you think you've fallen.

I will tie you down
so you can't resist.
Then I will kiss you,
merely kiss you.
From head to toe,
from lips to core.

You will feel my lips
on your throat.
You will feel my hands
across your body.
And you will feel me
deep inside —
even with night still young.

You and I
and a bottle of
whatever,
this night
can be ours
and the rest
of the world—
 it can wait.

Kiss me
 now
 and don't stop.

A bright
round moon
breaks through
the clouds,
and through her
I see
only you.

3 SENTENCES

A STUDY IN OBSESSION

Dance in the
moonlight
till icy sweat
tickles our
flesh.
  Close
  enough
  our hearts
  beat the
  same
  rhythm.
    Despite the snow, it gets indescribably hot.

Lost, she may be.
So reach out.
Bring her back.

Winter falls and darkness drops.
Take my hand.
I know the path to sunrise, but we
don't have to go there just yet.

I will kiss the back of your neck.
I will kiss the pulse of your wrist.
But I will most definitely kiss you, so be ready.

It's all but a dream.
A wish.
A perfect something.

We have shared an ocean.
We have shared a moon.
What might we share next?

Forged in fire like knives, she
rips apart barriers and shields.
She's too fierce to be stopped.
Why would you want to stop her?

You stand naked before me.
But none of your secrets are exposed.
You remain a delicious mystery.

I would write an ode to your beauty.
But we both know I'd get carried away
and say things I shouldn't.
So instead I'll just say hi, I had no idea
you are who you are, and I stand in awe
and surprise and pure joy.

Dance with me in those stockings.
I will hold you close.
I will learn how to move my hips.

She wears only weapons.
She would take something from you.
But you will surrender everything willingly.

You have my heart.
Maybe you'll wait
until I'm dead
and don't need it
before carving
up my chest
to add it
to your mantle.

But maybe
you can't wait.

I'm good
either way.

Sleep softly tonight.
I may drift
through your window
like a ghost.
I may tickle
the back of your neck
with my lips.

I didn't know
who I was
until I saw me
reflected
in your eyes.

Teach me, I say,
so you gouge my back
with your fingernails.
Tell me the truth, I say,
so you give me
silent smiles
and silent lies.
Love me, I say,
so you love me
thoroughly
in your broken way.
I relish the scars.

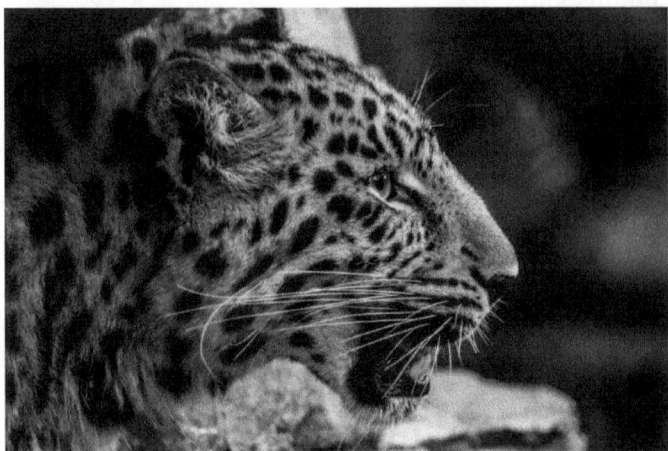

My dreams are shaped
like you and
smell like you
and taste
like
you.

It's your birthday
so I'm gonna
tie your wrists
to the corners of the bed,
stretch a silk blindfold
across your eyes,
use a Bowie knife
to cut free
everything you're wearing
that isn't lingerie
and leather harness.
I'll sign my name
across the tops
of your thighs
with my tongue,
then I'll ask
oh so very nicely
where you want
me to deliver
your birthday kiss.

Who knows what the night will bring?
We've got this chance here and now
and maybe never again. Let's dance.

You reminded me
    what it's like to love,
    what it's like to cry,
    what it's like
        to want things
        I cannot have.
And even when they hurt,
    these are lessons
    I need today
    if I want
        tomorrow.

You don't need me
to tell you you're beautiful
or amazing or incredible.
So when I tell you these things,
it's not so you
remember who you are.
It's so you remember how I see you.

I will cut off
a slice of my love
and serve it with
whipped cream
if you want,
chocolate sauce,
even a cherry.
I can serve it warm
with a scoop
of ice cream
on the side.
I'll even use
my own knife
unless you'd prefer
to use yours.

Poets talk of hearts,
but when I think of you
my gut churns.
When I touch you,
my blood burns.
When you whisper to me
promises and threats alike,
every nerve
is sensitized.

MOUNTAINS

Half a step
from an eight hundred foot
drop,
I stared
at the sunfall
on so many
rocky faces
and I
closed my eyes
to breathe.
I was alone
with the wind
and maybe my thoughts,
but I was trying
desperately
not to think.

This silence and
this darkness
are for you.
I'm here with you.
Take my hand
if you want.
Lay beside me.
Listen to the sounds
of your own breaths.
Think of nothing.
Think of everything.
This time is yours.
This space is yours.
And I'll hold you
or listen to you
or just breathe with you
or just be,
for you.

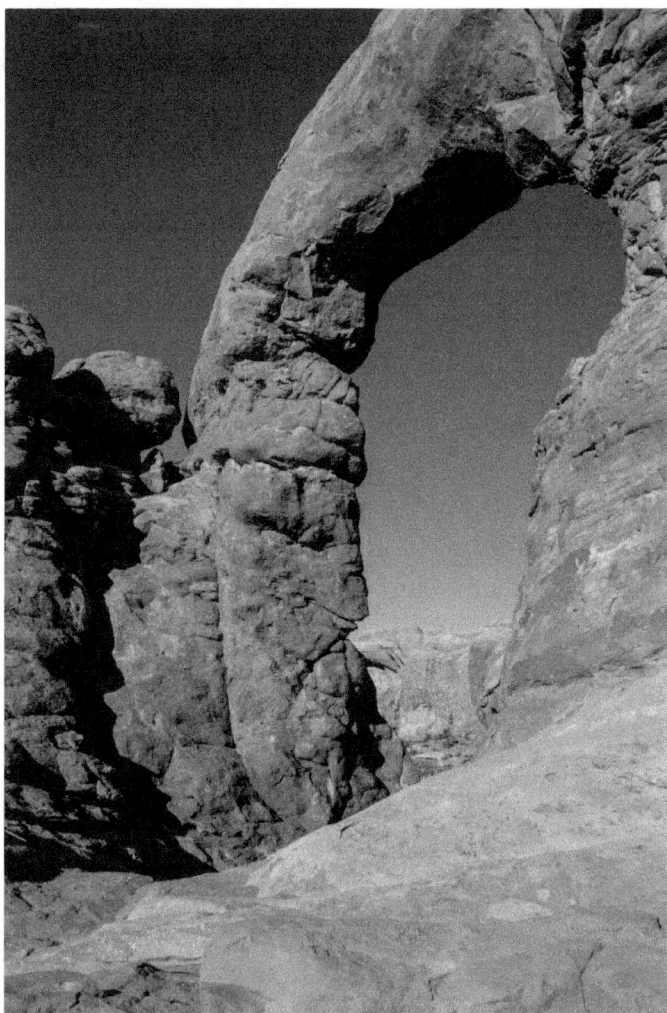

Sleep
is how we dream
and the only safe place
we can meet.
In dreams,
the knives aren't real,
the kisses insubstantial,
the poisons almost edible.
In dreams,
we can't be hurt
and we can't be
kept apart.
In waking,
I find myself alone
with fresh scars.

Vanilla drifts
through dreams
and I stop
where I stand
trying to discover
the source
but it's dark
and getting colder
and maybe
it's too late
to find you.

Silence
swirls
in anticipation
of the storm.

You are the dream
I've had
since I was a boy,
the one who would teach me
to ride a bicycle
without training wheels,
laughing when I fell
as you kissed the wounds
and licked the blood.
I never knew
what to make of you,
not even in dreams.

Invade my dreams tonight.
   Defend me
  from the nightmare shadows.
      Drift off to sleep in my arms
      after our victory champagne.

It's just
a dream kiss.
It isn't real.
I won't
suddenly
develop feelings
I never had.
Because
I've always
had them,
and nothing
has ever been
so real
as you and me
here and now
in this dream.

Those eyes.
Have you seen your own eyes?
And you wonder why my heart aches.

I spoke with the moon
the other night.
She told me secret things.
She said she'd show
you secrets, too.

A little bit of rain
is fine.
We can waltz
in the rain.
We can dance
near the river
with the ghosts,
and switch our rhythm
when the jazzmen
take over.
And when morning's light
begins to dissolve those mists,
we can retreat
to our rooms
and switch that rhythm
to something more private.
But the ghosts
will probably watch.

Lean closer
and tell me your secrets
in whispers.
Your hopes, which
I will try to gift to you.
Your fears, which
I will protect you from
if it costs me an eye,
a limb, or my life.
Your desires,
if you trust me with them.
You have nothing
to fear from me.
I know how swift
your blades can be.

I can be
good to you
and kind to you.
I can be nice to you
and I can be loving.
I can be quiet
when you need silence
and I can be a storm
when you need a tempest.
I can be yours,
if only for a short time,
or a long time if you prefer.
I will stand by you,
beside you, and behind you,
and even when you think
I've forgotten and moved on,
I can remember.

Give me another reason
to think the world of you.
I dare you.

Given time enough
to discover
the key
to your happiness,
I would waste
too many years
pursuing
ghosts and echoes
when all I should do
is tell you how much
I love you.

I want you to have
happiness.
I would love
to be responsible
for some of it.
But I want you to have it
regardless.

I will walk
  with you
anywhere.

Some nights,
there's no great quest,
no treasure to be won,
no heartache at risk.
It's just you
and me
and the moon,
quiet words
and gentle touches,
a comfortable darkness,
an unanticipated ease.
These are
the most intense depths
we'll ever know.

If you want to kiss me,

then kiss me.

I'm never

going to object.

Don't sit there

wondering

if I'll kiss you first.

I've never been

that daring,

even if you make me

want to be.

Volume I

The storm strikes
the shore relentlessly,
waves crashing
a hundred feet high
on rocks that
will shatter
even a siren's heart.
Thunder like
the quickened heartbeat
of a dying man
performing his final
heroic sacrifice.
Lightning bringing fire
and rain unending,
and the storm
rocks the very core
of the world.

Volume II

I tend to the flames,
trudging a hundred and seventy steps
with buckets full of oil
to keep the lighthouse lit,
a beacon and a warning
even through thickest storm
for all the brave sailors
and lonely captains
in their frigates and corvettes,
and for you
as good as alone
in a rowboat
trying to weather
Poseidon's ferocity.
I keep that light
so you might safely
navigate your
private maelstrom.

If I die
before I wake,
I loved you
more than
you know.

Tell me
truths
or lie to me,
just let me
hear
your voice.

Good night.
Dream well.
Know I'll be there
waiting
as always
with a kind word
and a kiss
and a sword in hand
to vanquish
any enemies
that dare intrude
on our private oasis.
And I'll be beside you
in the waking world
making certain
no one interrupts.
I'll hold you
until dawn breaks
a thousand times again.

Under
cover of darkness
provided by
the newest moon,
we dance
and whisper promises
we'll never
be allowed to keep
except
in dreams.

The moon is a goddess
of reflections.
If you and I look at her
at the same time
    —someone else can do the math
    on how long our gazes
    will take to bounce back—
at the same time,
it'll be like looking
into each other's eyes,
the fifteen hundred miles
between us
be damned.

I am a mystery
but the clues
have been laid out
before you.
I am meant
to be unraveled,
discovered,
solved,
and resolved.
All I need
is for you
to play sleuth.

DESERT

If you stray

    from the path

    you will be lost

        forever

        and quickly

        forgotten,

except maybe

from the dreams

of strangers

    whose eyes

    you momentarily burned.

        The storm clouds promise
        beauty like yours
        but I know you're not
        here or anywhere near.
        You're a voice echoing
        in memory and a picture
        fading on my phone.
        But I believe
        the promise.

It's you're birthday,
so a surprise kiss!
But I know
how you feel
about surprises,
so I'll warn you
it's coming;
and I know
how you feel
about kisses,
so it'll be
on the back of your neck
or your throat
or your wrist.
Maybe on your lips,
but maybe only if you
ask, beg, or demand...

I can tell you
   all the things I feel
      in poetry,
   then claim
      the poem wasn't
         written for you,
      but in my heart
         I hope
            you'll recognize
               the lie.

            I haven't any secrets.
            I'm a book,
            but difficult
            to get through.
            I'm badly edited,
            full of contradictions,
            dangling plot lines,
            and characters
            that simply
            disappeared.
            Don't become
            one of those.

An angel with broken wings
wanders the desert.
She drinks tequila
from any random cactus
and runs with coyotes.
They say she's mad,
but wouldn't you be?

Jazz musicians
take to the streets
and their guitars
leave holes in uncountable hearts
The poets ramble
and describe the scene
using words no one
dares comprehend.
The card readers
sit back and smile
and don't bother saying
they saw all this coming.

I don't know
what's next.
A challenge,
an obstacle,
maybe a mistake.
   It's not like
   I plan things
   anymore.

The moon promises
   to watch over us
   through all our trials
     against all the obstacles.
Yet once a month
   she leaves us
   on our own
     to watch over
     each other,
       to face our fears,
       and conquer
       our demons
         knowing the moon
           will come back
           to shine on us
           again.

A bright
round moon
breaks through
the clouds,
and through her
I see
only you.

A snake
making
promises
isn't as
impressive
as one
who keeps
them.

Every temptation
I've given in to
has left me here
on a rocky shore
surrounded by icy waters,
seal pups, and white sparrows
—drifting dreaming wishing—
but unable
to even remember
the sound
of your voice.

Secrets
aren't always
so dark.
Sometimes,
they're just
things forgotten.

You think you know
all my secrets
because I swore
I'd tell you
everything.
But you haven't
asked the questions,
you've hesitated to probe,
and you haven't learned
anything
that can't be found online.

You can't lose me.

    I don't disappear so easily.

    I'm not smoke

        drifting away.

I'm not infallible.

    I can be as quiet as you.

But the distance

    and the days

        months

        years

    mean nothing;

    if you call,

        I will answer.

Is this
where
the fairies
come to rest?

In the willow's shade
I dream
and in my dreams
I am beautiful
and so are you.

Of all the people,
I dream best
of you.

Hold me closely,
dance with me slowly,
tell me secrets
even if they're not true.

I thought
your eyes
would tell me
all the secrets,
reveal
your desires
and fears,
but it was your
trembling lips
when they touched
mine.

The storms
around you
only make you
beautiful.
And I
want to offer
a safe harbour.

Breath like ice,
but I'll
keep
you warm.

If you think
I want to write you
silly love poetics
dipped in romance,
you're right.
If you think
that requires
anything in return,
you're wrong.
The poetry is free.
But you are permitted
to give me words
in return.

I know it was only
a small kiss stolen
through a drunken haze.
I know it was
long ago and far away.
I can't forget
what should have followed.

In the darkest nights
I wander aimless
and lost
in search of something
I once had.
Sometimes the fog
is thick
or the snow
deep,
but on a clear night
when church bells sing
with the crickets,
I searched instead for you
—because once upon a time
   you promised me
   there were other things
   worth finding.

Ghosts
of sailors' wives
gather nightly
on their widows' walks
to watch the ocean
in anticipation
of men returning,
but they died
in the arms
of faraway
beauties.

I have a secret
I want you to know
but I'm afraid.

I saw the ghost
and I confess
she wore the
whitest lace.

> My heart skipped
> a beat,
> maybe two,
> and I knew
> my life was through.

>> But she smiled at me
>> with blood red lips,
>> then faded from my view.

I saw the ghost
and I confess
her mercy is why
I can tell you this.

I can change the ink
in a pen
more easily than
the blood in my veins.

No one can ever know you
in the ways I know you,
and they can never love you
with my strength,
my courage,
or my reckless abandon,
though they may want to
and you may want them to.
I will always remain
in a corner of your heart,
and I will always keep
a trace of your soul
for myself.
But I will let you go
and I will let you try,
and I will be here
when you're ready to come back.

I have secrets
that would topple
governments.
I can keep yours.

Have you ever had a secret
you never even
told to yourself?
Something that settles
in the back of memory
and emotion
to wait for a moment—
not necessarily a perfect moment
or always a good moment,
but the right moment—
for revelation?
And all you can think is,
"But this was never my secret."
Maybe that secret
was implanted in your past
only today
to force the question:
will you keep this secret
or act on it?

A thousand miles
and more
keep us apart,
but we look
upon the same moon
to make our wishes.

First breath
of the morning
but there's no sun.
We'll dance
in the rain instead
and dream up
new memories.

HIGHWAY

The road,
it leads me elsewhere:
  to golden forests
  to rusty deserts
    ancient theaters
    ocean shipwrecks.
But the road
will never lead me
  back to you.

The ocean stretches
beyond that horizon
to foreign lands
filled with mythical people
and ghosts.
It looks dark
in the night
because the night is dark,
but beyond that horizon
the sun has already risen
and the ghosts rejoice
in your new day
yet unseen.

Around a bend
in the road
I was bathed
in golden light
and golden shadows
under a golden
fairy tale canopy,
and I realized
my vision
had been unnecessarily
fettered.

I think of you
too much
but only in the best ways.

My cat
        doesn't like you.
He prefers
        my undivided
                attention.

I don't dream often
of trivial things.
The occasional nightmare
intrudes,
and sometimes ghosts,
memories, and forgotten
heartbreaks.
When I control
my dreams,
like ordering room service,
I only ask for you.

In dreams
    we dance
    and sing
    and walk
        through darkness and day.
    We stand together
    and wander together
    and get lost
        on the streets
        of exotic cities.
We hold hands
    and we kiss
    and we share secrets
        without many words.
    Those few
        we share
        are brilliant.
Even in our shared dreams
    I dream
    of such a life
    outside of dreams.

Your eyes
see through
the lies I tell myself,
the masks I wear
even when I think
I'm vulnerable.
You point out the flaws
in my defenses
so I can better
protect myself
but also because
you know
you're on the inside
and nothing I do,
not even the things
I do intentionally,
will ever
change
that.

Blissfully ignorant
of horrors beneath,
I kill the engines
and drift on the
Atlantic swell.

Mysteries of the waters call
when you walk the shores.
Sirens beckon.
Treasures await.
And also death,
in its many
unfathomable
forms.

Our love
is an ocean,
the tides
ever changing it,
always in motion,
sometimes calm and
sometimes tumultuous,
always vast,
impossible
to ever see
the whole of,
different
every day,
and subject
to the whims
of the moon.

OCEAN

I'm brewing poison again
hoping you'll want a taste
but of course it's for me,
it's always for me,
though we've both
built up
an immunity.

A day came
when I had
nothing
left to give,
no strength
to push forward,
no breath
to take.
But the promise
off your lips
got me
to move.

I'll clear away
the monsters
so you can
wake refreshed
and unharmed
from every dream
that makes you happy.

In a forest
fairy tale world
I will eat the apple
and barter with trolls
to cross the bridge,
I will follow
the lights
and stray off the path,
I will listen
to the sirens sing
and ignore the warnings
of Icarus and Orpheus,
and I will offer
the witch the meal
she craves most
if it will
bring you back.

FOREST

A canopy
of golden leaves
protects us
from what's real.

I'm tired.
The road has been long
and there's no knowing
how many more miles
await.
I have fought
your demons
and bruised my fists
but I cannot
deliver the killing blow.
Only you can.
But today, you won't
or you can't,
or you're tired, too.
I'll return tomorrow
to fight for you
again.
Just like so many
yesterdays.

If I wanted
   to build
      the perfect person
I would take
   your eyes
   because they see me
   in ways
   I've never felt seen.
I would take
   your legs,
   because you're a dancer
   with poise and grace
   and unshakable balance.
I would take
   your hands to hold.
I would give her
   your thoughts
   and memories,
   even the hard ones,
   because they make you
   who you are.
And also your lips
   to kiss.

If I had
a dream of you,
I might decide
not to wake.

It's the end of a long journey
but that doesn't mean
I'm done.
Questions remain unanswered.
Anxiety has arrived
where it never existed before
and nobody knows what's next.
The world is ending
around me,
but all I can think of
is you.

I wrote a story once
too true,
and I bled for it
and I cried.
When I was done,
you shut the book
and asked,
"What's next?"
Because the story lied
when it came to a conclusion.

After sunset,
it's all indigo
deeper
into the night,
but you look fine
by indigo lights
and I don't need
to see you
to hold your hand,
to hear your voice,
to feel your breath.

Nothing
hurts
forever.
We won't
live that long.

Her song
is inescapable,
and I forget
why I wanted
to escape.

Don't think of this
as an ending.
There's no such thing.
Even the stories
that end happily
ever after
still have
an ever after.

ACKNOWLEDGMENTS

This is not a book about how to heal. This isn't about how I healed—I'm not fully healed, not yet, maybe not ever. It's just a snapshot of my healing process.

Mary Lescher was my partner for over two decades and across three continents. After she died, I wandered the United States, borrowing beds and couches in Pennsylvania, Ohio, Michigan, Illinois, Iowa, Nebraska, Colorado, Utah, Idaho, Washington, Oregon, California, Arizona, Texas, Arkansas, Tennessee, and Florida. In a very real way, as I write this, I am still wandering. The photos in this book, with the exception of Mary at the start, are exclusively from this odyssey.

Parts of this book may seem to have nothing to do with Mary. But make no mistake: the memory of her, the love we shared, and the life we lived are everywhere.

I have been fortunate to discover that I have extraordinary taste in friends, and I got a chance to see many of them on this odyssey. I also saw things I never would have seen and experienced wonders I'd never imagined. This book would not have been possible without all of you.

As always, a special thanks to Sabine and the Rose Fairy. You will always be with me.

PHOTOGRAPHY

All photos shot by John Urbancik
except Mary Lescher's portrait,
which was found at her parents' house

Page 5 – Hollywood Forever Cemetery, California

Page 14 – near Kennewick, Washington

Page 26 – near Astoria, Oregon

Page 29 – Lake Michigan

Page 36 – San Diego Zoo

Page 40,41 – Rocky Mountain National Park;
    and Colorado National Monument

Page 43 – Arches National Park, Utah

Page 49 – Moltnomah Falls, Oregon

Page 60 – Colorado National Monument

Page 62,63 – Arches National Park, Utah;
    and outside El Paso, Texas

Page 68 – near Carlsbad Cavern National Park, New
    Mexico

Page 73 – outside El Paso, Texas

Page 76 – Carlsbad Caverns, New Mexico

Page 81 – undisclosed location, Pennsylvania

Page 83 – Susquehanna River, Pennsylvania

Page 86 – highway near Boulder, Colorado

Page 87 – Golden Gate Bridge

Page 93, 93 – Pacific Ocean near Astoria, Oregon

Page 96 – near Peoria, Illinois

Page 97 – near Little Rock, Arkansas

Page 107 – Self Portrait in Portland, Oregon 2014.

ABOUT THE PROJECT AND AUTHOR

John Urbancik's business card proclaims him a Writer, Photographer, and Adventurer. Lately, he's leaned heavily into the Adventurer part of that, hitting the road to wander the United States like a nomad, vagabond, and tramp for the last half of 2019 and into 2020. As this is being written and published, there are only tentative plans for what happens next. A good bet would be on more words following.

He was born on a small island in the northeast United States called Manhattan. He and his partner, Mary Lescher, had lived together in Orlando and Tallahassee, Florida; Sydney, Australia; Richmond, Virginia; and Madrid, Spain. Mary Lescher passed away in the summer of 2019. John Urbancik's future, as ever, remains unwritten.

ALSO BY JOHN URBANCIK

NOVELS
Sins of Blood and Stone
Breath of the Moon
Once Upon a Time in Midnight
Stale Reality
The Corpse and the Girl from Miami
DarkWalker 1: Hunting Grounds
DarkWalker 2: Inferno
DarkWalker 3: The Deep City
DarkWalker 4: Armageddon
DarkWalker 5: Ghost Stories
DarkWalker 6: Other Realms
Choose Your Doom

NOVELLAS
A Game of Colors
The Rise and Fall of Babylon (with Brian Keene)
Wings of the Butterfly
House of Shadow and Ash
Necropolis
Quicksilver
Beneath Midnight
Zombies vs. Aliens vs. Robots vs. Cowboys vs.
Ninja vs. Investment Bankers vs. Green Berets
Colette and the Tiger
Madmen, Poets & Thieves
Clockwork Ravens
The Night Carnival

COLLECTIONS
Shadows, Legends & Secrets
Sound and Vision
Tales of the Fantastic and the Phantasmagoric

POETRY
John the Revelator

NONFICTION
InkStained: On Creativity, Writing, and Art

INKSTAINS
Multiple volumes